MW00640209

SHATTERED DREAMS

What To Do
When Your Future Seems Lost

By Robb Thompson

WHAT OTHERS ARE SAYING ABOUT SHATTERED DREAMS

Read *Shattered Dreams* not once, but many times until the Holy Spirit causes its contents to become revelation to your spirit. God has given Robb Thompson the unique ability to present the truths from the Word of God that will help you enjoy the fulfillment of your dreams.

> *Evangelist Jerry Savelle*
> *Jerry Savelle Ministries*
> *International*
> *Crowley, Texas*

There are too many people who hate what they do because their dreams have been shattered. They do not live; they simply exist. This book by Robb Thompson will help you take the steps necessary to get your dreams back. After reading *Shattered Dreams*, I didn't just feel like *facing* tomorrow; I felt like taking it hostage!

> *Dave Roberson*
> *Pastor, The Family Prayer Center*
> *Tulsa, Oklahoma*

Unless otherwise indicated, all Scripture quotations are taken from the *New King James Version*, copyright © 1982 by Thomas Nelson, Inc. All rights reserved.

Scripture quotations marked *KJV* are taken from the *King James Version* of the Bible.

Scripture quotations marked *AMP* are taken from *The Amplified Bible. Old Testament* copyright © 1965, 1987 by Zondervan Corporation, Grand Rapids, Michigan. New Testament copyright © 1958, 1987 by The Lockman Foundation, La Habra, California. All rights reserved.

Scripture quotations marked *NIV* are taken from the *Holy Bible: New International Version®. NIV®.* Copyright © 1973, 1978, 1984 by International Bible Society. Used by permission of Zondervan Publishing House. All rights reserved.

Shattered Dreams:
What To Do When Your Future Seems Lost
ISBN 1-889723-23-1
Copyright © 2002 by Robb Thompson
Family Harvest Church
18500 92nd Ave.
Tinley Park, Illinois 60477

Third Printing, 2003

Editorial Consultant: Cynthia Hansen
Text Design: Lisa Simpson
Cover Design: Greg Lane

Printed in the United States of America.
All rights reserved under International Copyright Law.
Contents and/or cover may not be reproduced in whole or in part in any form without the express written consent of the Publisher.

TABLE OF CONTENTS

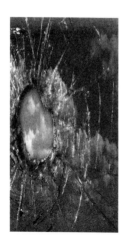

Chapter **1**

RESTORING YOUR DREAM:

Finding Riches In the Ruins

As far as I am concerned, God turned into good what you meant for evil. He brought me to the high position I have today so I could save the lives of many people....

— Genesis 50:20 *NLT*

"We Christians are not called to respond to criticism; we are called to respond to God."

— *John Mason*

Throughout the course of history, men and women have fought, cried, and struggled against both people and circumstances, trying to keep their dreams from being stolen from them before those dreams could be realized. Many of these individuals have succeeded against seemingly hopeless odds.

- Marathon runner Joan Benoit underwent painful knee surgery only seventeen days before the U. S. Olympic trials. Nevertheless, she went on to win the first-ever U. S. Olympic gold medal in the event.

- Michelangelo spent seven years on his back — often blinded by searing paint dripping into his eyes — as he painted his breathtaking masterpiece within the Sistine Chapel in Rome.

- Inventor Charles Carlson hit the lonely streets for years before anyone would take his Xerox photocopying process seriously.

The list goes on and on. Unfortunately, the list of those who succeeded against the odds is dwarfed by the far longer list of those who failed miserably to achieve their dreams. This latter list is tragic testimony to the millions of history's unnamed and forgotten people who simply gave up, frustrated and defeated by a world where dreams are often trampled, tossed out, and destroyed.

Over the years, I've learned that shattered dreams are far more common than you might imagine. Great ideas, passions, careers, and callings have all been lost for reasons too difficult to define.

For almost two decades, my pastoral ministry has reached thousands of people who believed their dreams had been irrevocably shattered. I've always been amazed at the vast number of men and women who have approached me in a spirit of fear and defeat, absolutely sure that God Himself had shattered their dreams and left them without hope for the future.

But as you read this book, I want you to consider another possibility, a possibility far greater and more powerful than any defeat, humiliation, or loss. Consider the possibility that no matter what dream has been shattered in your life, it can be not only *recovered*, but *restored and given new life*.

God's Perspective
On Restoration

God very much wants you to realize this possibility in your own life. However, before you can do that, you must first be willing to take a long, hard look at your present situation through the eyes of His Word.

For instance, have you ever read God's perspective regarding *restoration?* Exodus 22:3 says that a thief must certainly make restitution. Proverbs 6:31 says that if a thief is caught, he must repay sevenfold what he has stolen. And in Joel 2:25, God says, **"So I will restore to you the years that the swarming locust has eaten...."**

In today's society, we have all but forgotten what restoration is all about. Today when a person commits a crime, he may still profit from that crime even if he goes to jail, selling the rights to his story for hundreds of thousands of dollars. But what about the victim of the crime?

Our current legal system seems to have forgotten about the biblical principle of bringing restoration to the victim. According to the book of Proverbs, the criminal is to restore to the victim as much as seven times what he took from that person!

But we haven't just forgotten about the principle of restoration in our legal system; we have also forgotten about it in our personal lives. However, *God* hasn't forgotten. He wants to restore everything the thief — especially the worst thief of all, Satan himself — has taken from us.

Therefore, we must sear into our consciousness that *God is interested in restoration* and that one of His greatest priorities is restoring the dreams that the enemy has shattered in our lives.

The Shattered Dreams Of Our Past

So let me ask you this: Do you remember the dreams you had as a young person that sent you soaring through your young life like an eagle? I'm not talking about those childhood desires to grow up and become a fireman, a nurse, an astronaut, or a ballerina. I'm talking about the dreams that probably started around high school or college — the dreams you realistically believed in and hoped one day to achieve. Perhaps they were dreams that God Himself dropped into your heart.

I spent many of my early years in the 1960s, growing up in the generation that produced the hippies, the flower children, the peace movement, and free love. In those days, we believed we could do anything. In fact, we thought we were true world-changers, completely invincible and almost immortal. Looking back, however, I realize now that we were grasping for something that didn't exist — something that had no real substance.

That's why my dreams eventually crashed and burned. The day my dreams finally abandoned me, I landed in a mental hospital, tormented by thoughts that said my life, career, marriage, and bid for success in life were over as quickly as they had begun.

The story of how God touched my life in that terrible situation — completely delivering me and then calling me to preach the Gospel — is another book. (You can read my testimony in greater detail in my book *The Great Exchange: Your Thoughts for God's Thoughts*). But the bottom line is this: When I was struggling through the most horrible circumstances of my life, God didn't forget me. And when I finally opened my heart to His healing and delivering touch in my life, that broken, defeated life was given new direction and purpose. Finally, I had a real reason to go on.

Since that time, the more I talk to people, the more I realize that every person has been through the same experience to one degree or another — even you.

Oh, you may not have lived through the 1960s; you may never have been admitted to a mental hospital; and you may never have wanted to commit suicide like I once did. But chances are that your dreams were dashed at some time in your past. Perhaps your life became nothing more than a series of compromises as you settled for less than the best again and again. As a result, you may have given up, deciding that your dream wasn't worth further effort. In fact, you may have even resigned yourself to the notion that everything you used to desire was all just a bad, unrealistic dream (or a nightmare!).

Every time I meet someone who fits this description, I'm reminded of a quote by internationally known real estate developer Trammel Crow. Crow once stated, *"There's as much risk in doing nothing as in doing something."*

I'm convinced it takes nearly as much courage to lose as it does to win. However, there is one big difference: Winning is linked to the fear of the unknown, whereas the obstacles that cause people to lose *are* well known. In fact, those obstacles are long-time foes that surround mankind every day, hindering the progress of multitudes of people, such as:

11

- The taxi driver who once dreamed of driving a winning race car.

- The salesman who once dreamed of becoming a famous senator.

- The secretary who once dreamed of becoming a great actress.

- The Sunday school teacher who once dreamed of becoming a pioneering missionary.

How about you? Have your dreams been crushed in the past? Did you once have aspirations of greatness, only to have the circumstances of life or the people close to you shatter those dreams to pieces?

If you are honest with yourself, you more than likely would have to admit that as a child, you had aspirations of being something truly great when you grew to be an adult. Even today, you know deep down inside that God has called you to greatness. You can feel it, taste it, smell it. But at one time or another, those dreams of greatness you once cherished were crushed and finally abandoned along the wayside of life.

A Common 'Dream-Destroyer': Other People's Discouraging Words

Too many of our dreams are destroyed because of negative things that other people say. In fact, almost every failure you and I have ever experienced was due to the programming we received from our parents, teachers, ministers, friends, enemies, or employers.

For instance, someone close to a person may tell him that he will never make the grade — that he doesn't have what it takes to succeed. If that person accepts those words as truth, he will eventually stop believing in the dreams he has been nurturing in his heart. Jesus said in Mark 9:23 (*NIV*), **"...Everything is possible for him who believes."** But what about those who *don't* believe?

Of course, there are other reasons that dreams are dashed. Some people experience accidents that cause physical disability. In some cases, timing, finances, or circumstances beyond people's control cause their dreams to be set back or defeated.

But through the years, I've discovered that *most people are not victims of circumstances.* More often than not, their dreams are destroyed because they believe other people's discouraging words.

Face it! Criticism, ridicule, and verbal abuse hurts. I remember this quote in the *Wall Street Journal*: "When you make your mark in the world, look out for people with erasers." Sadly, our strongest critics are often the ones closest to us.

Sir Basic Spencer, the brilliant British architect, reported that he received 700 letters regarding his remarkable design for the new cathedral in Coventry, England. He stated, "Eighty percent were rude, and the other twenty percent were very rude."

At the peak of Abraham Lincoln's popularity, he once said: "If I tried to read, much less answer, all the criticisms made of me and all the attacks leveled against me, this office would have to be closed for all other business."

Day after day, people criticize us, humiliate us, verbally abuse us, and ridicule us, often causing us to give up or settle for less. But the fact is, God doesn't want us to settle for that kind of defeat. As Harry Gray, a very successful business executive, once said, *"No one ever achieved greatness by playing it safe."*

The Bible is full of stories of people just like you and me who beat the odds and overcame the external opposition and criticism that came against them. These were people who led lives of victory, power, and effectiveness because they learned to put God's Word into action and eliminate the destructive influences others exerted over their lives. These individuals chose to see beyond the vicious spirits that were trying to defeat them and move into a realm of limitless possibilities — the realm of God and His grace.

A Man Who Beat the Odds

Let's look at what the Bible says about one particular man who not only beat the odds, but also defeated the criticism of his family and any subsequent feelings of guilt.

You see, God didn't create mankind to be controlled by guilt. First Corinthians 6:11 tells us that we are washed and made free from the terrible guilt of sin. Romans 8:1 confirms this when it says, **"There is therefore now no condemnation to those who are in Christ Jesus...."**

This man I want to talk about was also able to beat society's "victim mentality" — a malady that is becoming more and more common in modern society. So many people walk around today thinking that they are victims. But in most cases, the reason these people are in the mess they're in is that they refused to say no to the status quo of a merciless society.

Some people blame their lack of success on a bad childhood, on bad teachers or coaches, or even on bad friends. I could have used this excuse myself because prior to my parents' encounter with the King of kings, they were very fond of drinking.

Some people say, "The reason I'm not where I want to be in life is that other people have kept me from being great. Because of that, I deserve help in making a better life — in getting a job, more money, and just about everything else." These people think that society owes them everything. They're going to get all they can, and no one is going to stop them. "You owe me!" they proclaim. "You owe me because of what you did to me." Sometimes these accusations evolve from slights that are generations old.

The man we are preparing to study beat all these problems — the guilt trips, the criticism of his family, and society's victim mentality — and went on to become the second most powerful man in the world. What is the name of this remarkable man? *Joseph.*

Seeds of Deception
Produce a Negative Harvest

Before we look at Joseph's life, however, it's important to go back a generation and examine his father Jacob. Jacob's story begins in Genesis 25. So you can better understand this discussion, I encourage you to read chapters 25 through 50 in the book of Genesis.

In fact, let me say this as an aside: I strongly suggest that you begin a daily pattern of reading the Word of God and meditating on its personal applications to your life. *Don't be like so many others who try to apply the Word to their lives. Instead, rise above the crowd and apply your life to the Word!*

Also, don't be afraid to mark your Bible! My Bible has notes in the margins, in the front and back, and just about anywhere else space exists. Why? Because I believe it's important for us to instantly take notes as we read so we can go back later and remember the insights and thoughts God brought to our minds during that time.

Psalm 119:18 (*NIV*) says, **"Open my eyes that I may see wonderful things in your law."** Then in Ephesians 1:17 (*NIV*), Paul says, **"I keep asking that the God of our Lord Jesus Christ, the glorious Father, may give you the Spirit of wisdom and revelation, so that you may know him better."** These scriptures make it clear that it is God's desire that you study His Word. In return, He will enlighten you so you can know Him better.

So begin applying these principles of Bible study right now as you read this book. As you do, God will start to open new avenues of insight and inspiration to the obstacles and problems you may be facing in your life.

As you read about Jacob beginning in Genesis 25, you'll notice that throughout the earlier years of his life, he was a very crafty, cunning individual. You probably remember that he deceitfully cheated his brother Esau out of his birthright as a firstborn son. Afterward, Jacob had to go on the run because he was afraid his brother was going to kill him. In great fear, Jacob left his home and traveled to his uncle Laban's house, escaping what he thought would be a certain and miserable death at the hands of his cheated brother.

During this time, Jacob met Rachel, his uncle's daughter, and immediately fell in love. So Jacob asked Laban, "What must I do to have Rachel as my wife?

Laban replied, "You must serve me for seven years, working on my farm in return for Rachel."

However, Jacob had no idea that his uncle was as crafty and cunning as he was himself. Jacob served Laban for seven grueling years. At the end of those seven long years, the family finally held the long-anticipated wedding.

If held according to the customs of the time, the wedding was probably a splendid, elaborate affair. Later when it was time for the marriage to be consummated, Jacob went into his tent in great expectation and made love to the woman he thought was his Rachel. But when he woke up the next morning, he discovered that his new wife wasn't Rachel at all, but rather her sister Leah.

Uncle Laban knew that Leah wasn't as pretty as Rachel and that Jacob loved Rachel more than anything else on earth. So Laban devised a way to extract seven more years of work out of Jacob by secretly switching brides on him. Jacob, the great con artist, had been conned himself!

I have to admit that it's difficult to comprehend how Jacob could have been deceived like this, but it happened. Jacob was stuck with a wife he didn't want because of the universal principle stated in Galatians 6:7 (*NIV*): **"Do not be deceived: God cannot be mocked. A man reaps what he sows."**

Jacob had known Rachel's sister Leah for seven years. He knew who she was, and he knew one thing better than he knew anything else — he wanted no part of

17

her. Nevertheless, he had spent the night in her bridal bed and was therefore bound to her for the rest of his life.

When Jacob woke up the next morning, he no doubt went steaming to his father-in-law and shouted, *"You tricked me!"*

Laban replied in his deceitful, pitiful way, "Oh, forgive me."

Jacob said, "Now, wait a second. You were supposed to give me Rachel as my wife."

Laban shot back a quick response: "Well, I'll make you a deal. Serve me seven more years, and I'll arrange for Rachel to be your wife."

At that point, Jacob was stuck according to the Law, so he reluctantly agreed. The customs of the time allowed Jacob to have not only Leah as his wife, but Leah's maidservant as well. And after Jacob agreed to the terms of Laban's bargain, he would also have Rachel and Rachel's servant as his wives as well. (Actually, that isn't very different from today's permissive society — one man with four women!)

So there was Jacob — one husband with four wives, and all the while he was only in love with Rachel. I imagine he probably took Rachel aside in the moonlight and said, "Sweetheart, you're the only one I love. I'm not interested in anyone else but you. You are the greatest!"

Meanwhile, the other three wives knew exactly how Jacob felt.

After agreeing to Laban's terms to work for him another seven years, Jacob finally got his wish, and he and Rachel were married. Jacob's other wives did everything they could to frame poor Rachel and make her look bad in the eyes of her husband. They also did everything they could to gain Jacob's acceptance and love. But their efforts were all to no avail, and they therefore hated Rachel with a passion.

Then the three unloved wives of Jacob hit on an idea. Knowing how highly prized children were in their culture, all three of them worked on getting pregnant. Soon all of Jacob's wives except Rachel were expecting children. For whatever reason, Rachel just couldn't have a child.

The other pride-filled mothers used their babies to try to win their husband's affection. But Jacob's deepest affection was still toward Rachel. He loved her, wanted her, and needed her. She remained his first love.

Finally, God saw Rachel's tears and heard her prayers, and the day came when Rachel got pregnant. Nine months later, she gave birth to a little baby boy and named him Joseph. Jacob was so happy. Oh, how he loved Joseph!

But many years had passed by then. Joseph's brothers were old enough to be his father, and they hated him with a jealous passion just as their mothers hated Rachel. Joseph was the only one of the brothers to ever receive an education; the only one their father really adored; and the only one who stood between them and their father's inheritance. Perhaps worst of all in their eyes, Joseph was given the coat of the firstborn, which symbolized his position as the family manager.

God's Covenant
Was His Commitment

You know, it's interesting that when we talk about the patriarchs, we often think of a bunch of holy men sitting around talking about holy (and mostly boring) things. But in fact, nothing could be further from the truth.

The patriarchs were hardened men. Wind-blown, tough, and rugged, they were driven by the harsh realities of the desert. They were men with matted, long beards, rough dispositions, and deadly weapons strapped to their sides. They were men who feared God and who lived under the constant threat of the sword. It's difficult to understand today the pressure, customs, and rules they built their lives on. But I can assure you that their lives weren't easy. The Bible doesn't pull any punches when it talks about their mistakes, shortcomings, and failures.

That's why the Bible is such a wonderful book. It tells it like it is.

The patriarchs were men who could raise a sword and defend themselves and their families, but they were also men who had a covenant relationship with God. Remember, *God's covenant was God's commitment.* God's covenant was His demonstration of the New Testament concept of *agape* love for His people. It was God saying, "This is what I will do for you." And it didn't matter what God's people did to violate their covenant with Him; God's commitment to them remained unchanged.

You see, God doesn't change His commitment when we change ours. Second Timothy 2:13 reminds us that even when we are faithless, God will remain faithful. He will never deny His faithfulness. Because of the covenant He has made with us, God says, *"This is what I am going to do for you."*

I don't know where people get the idea that God is saying to them, "You do something for me, and I'll do something for you. One hand washes the other, so you scratch my back, and I'll scratch yours." Many people believe that God works that way, but nothing could be further from the truth. God says in His Word, "As far as I'm concerned, this is what I'll do for you. Now it's up to you to either believe or disbelieve what I've promised."

A Brother Betrayed

Jacob was very grateful that God had finally given him a son through his first love Rachel, and Jacob dearly loved Joseph. By the time Joseph was seventeen years of age, it was evident that he had a powerful intellect. In fact, Jacob even had Joseph running the family business! I'm sure Jacob couldn't have been more proud.

One day when Joseph was on his way out to the field where his brothers tended their flocks, his brothers saw him in the distance. As the brothers watched Joseph approach, they started to have a discussion about him.

One of the brothers said, "I hate him. I just hate him!"

The rest of them chimed in, "Yes, things would be better for all of us if he were out of the way." (You can see how much they wanted to destroy Joseph.)

Then Reuben, the oldest brother, stood up and said, "No, you're not going to kill him. You can't go that far." But Reuben couldn't completely foil his brothers' plan, so they finally reached an agreement to capture Joseph and throw him in a pit.

That way, the brothers reasoned, Joseph's blood wouldn't be on *their* hands. Perhaps he would die of starvation and exposure, but at least they wouldn't have actually killed him. In their distorted minds, they could honestly say to all who questioned them that they had nothing to do with their brother's disappearance.

You can see how clouded people's minds get when they feed on hatred and jealousy! It sounds like the twisted thinking you hear so much today, doesn't it? For instance, the people today who fight hardest for animal rights are the ones who want abortion on demand!

I actually saw an advertisement recently for an AIDS organization that used the rallying cry, *"Choose life!"* There is no question that AIDS is a terrible disease and that we should do everything in our power to stop it. But I find it interesting that those very people crying, *"Choose life!"* during an AIDS campaign turn their backs on that same cry when it comes in support of unborn children. It seems that society's "majority rules" system is constructed in this way. The natural is always called upon to finance the unnatural.

One of the most piercingly honest statements I ever read was a prolife advertising billboard that said, "It shouldn't happen to a dog, but it's okay to do it to a baby." Perhaps the kind of twisted thinking that billboard is referring to isn't so new after all. Obviously, people in Joseph's day twisted the circumstances to suit their circumstances as well.

The brothers threw Joseph down in a pit; then they stripped off his coat of many colors. That coat was the most prized gift Joseph's father had ever given him. But it had become a symbol to Joseph's brothers of their violent hatred for him and of their father's favoritism toward him.

It's interesting to note that the phrase "coat of many colors" didn't actually mean it was multi-colored. A coat of many colors was actually a robe that was made up of many different pieces of cloth. It was most likely longer than any of the other robes the rest of the brothers wore. It also had a tassel down at the bottom, which was supposed to symbolize the firstborn of a family.

Notice that the one whom Jacob loved most was his *last* born, not his firstborn. Joseph was to receive the portion usually reserved for his oldest brother, Reuben. *And the older brothers hated Jacob for that.*

Of course, the ten brothers could never get away with hating their father. They would never come against their own father because in their culture, that just wasn't acceptable. So Jacob's older sons took an alternate route. They saved their hatred for the one their father loved the most. They plotted and schemed against Joseph in order to make themselves look better in the eyes of their father.

(Don't say you've never done that. Every one of us has done something similar at one time or another. We may not have known we were doing it, but we did it nonetheless.)

So the brothers stripped off Joseph's clothes and threw him in a pit. They thought they were doing this to get rid of "father's pet." *But they were really trying to kill Joseph because of his dream.*

Amid Joseph's desperate shouts and pleas for mercy, the brothers sat down, built a campfire, and discussed what to do next. Some wanted to go ahead and destroy Joseph. They argued back and forth by the dim light of the glowing campfire:

"Come on, let's kill him. Let's get rid of this brat once and for all."

"Oh, I don't know if we should do that. Maybe we should just leave him in the pit."

"No, let's do away with him. He's good for nothing. He's stolen everything that rightfully belongs to us!"

"That's right — he's taken everything that belongs to me. Now let's destroy him!"

Hearing the argument, Joseph cried out from the pit, "No, no! Don't do this to me. Come and get me out of this pit, and please forgive me. I'm your little brother! Don't leave me here to die!"

But the brothers yelled back, "No, we're finally going to be rid of you!"

Then by the hand of God, a caravan of gypsies passed by the brothers' camp as they sat around arguing with each other about Joseph. The newcomers were actually members of a tribe called the Ishmaelites. They were known to buy anything from anybody.

"A slave for a good price? We'll take him!"

So the brothers pulled Joseph up from the pit and paraded him in front of the Ishmaelites. "He has good skin and good teeth; he's intelligent and a hard worker. He'll make a good slave," the brothers boasted.

Joseph continued his desperate pleading: "Don't turn me in. Don't sell me away. I love you all. Have mercy — I'm your brother!"

Joseph's brothers heard him cry out for mercy, but they gave him none.

Have you ever been victimized by your own family? Have you ever been abused or taken advantage of by those who were closest to you, those who were supposed to care for you, those whom you trusted and loved? If so, you can probably relate to how Joseph must have felt on that dark day.

Sin triumphed that day in the camp of Jacob's sons. Joseph's own brothers successfully sold him to the Ishmaelites.

Life as an Egyptian Slave

We know this story is based in fact even beyond the biblical record. Other historical records indicate how Ishmaelites treated the people they bought on their way down to Egypt, where they always found a market for slaves. According to these records, we know that the Ishmaelites probably bound Joseph with ropes in a very uncomfortable sitting position, his bent knees pressed tightly to his body right under his chin. Then they transported him in a wicker basket that hung on the side of one of their camels.

Historical records also tell us about the trade route the Ishmaelites traveled from that region of the Middle East all the way to Egypt. In fact, scholars believe that this particular caravan may have gone right past Jacob's house in order to reach Egypt. Imagine — Joseph may have even seen his father's house in the distance as he was being transported as human merchandise to Egypt!

Today many people have the idea that Joseph was some sort of special case. They think Joseph was the kind of person for whom good things just sort of happened. He just got the lucky ticket. Everything the young man did turned sorrow into gold. They assume that everything in Joseph's life eventually turned out right.

But that is simply not true. He was seventeen years old, running his father's business with the world in the palm of his hand. But now within a matter of hours he was being transported as a slave to a country that hated and despised his kind.

Now what was he to do?

Rejected, dejected, abandoned, and hated, young Joseph was taken to Egypt to live the rest of his life as a slave. But as the old saying goes, *"The size of a dog in a fight is not as significant as the size of the fight in the dog!"*

When Joseph was taken to Egypt, he was immediately sold to a very wealthy man named Potiphar. After Potiphar bought Joseph, he could see very quickly that the young man was exceptionally intelligent and that everything Joseph touched seemed to prosper. He may not have realized that the hand of the Lord was on his young slave. But Potiphar did notice that there was something special about him, so it wasn't long before the Egyptian master put Joseph in charge of his entire household (Gen. 39:2-4).

God Is Ever With You

We find many cases in Joseph's life where the Bible says, "And the Lord was with Joseph." (Actually, you will find this to be true throughout the book of Genesis.)

So even if you've been victimized or abused, remember that God is always with you. He is always protecting you. Can you fathom how bad it might have been through the years had God *not* been protecting you from others and from yourself?

You still might ask, "But why did God let those negative things happen?" He didn't. The terrible things that happen in this world are not the result of a God who randomly decides to inflict pain on desperate and hurting people. Those tragedies are the result of a fallen world that became broken when man chose the way of sin and death over God's way of goodness and love. Because of that choice, God hurts as much as we do as He waits for people to cry out to Him so He can reach into their broken circumstances with healing and restoration.

Remember Romans 8:22 and 23:

> **For we know that the whole creation groans and labors with birth pangs together until now.**
> **Not only that, but we also who have the first-fruits of the Spirit, even we ourselves groan within ourselves, eagerly waiting for the adoption, the redemption of our body.**

The fact is that even in your worst moment, God was there all the time. In fact, He said in Hebrews 13:6 that He would *never* leave you nor forsake you. He is always there to help you and to bring you to a place of forgiveness regarding those who have perpetrated evil against you.

It was the same with Joseph. Even after he was sold as a slave to Potiphar, the Lord's hand continued to be upon him. Despite the difficult circumstances Joseph found himself in, he kept rising to the top. Soon he was running Potiphar's household — a household so large that Potiphar didn't even know what or how much he owned (Gen. 39:6)! Joseph was taking care of everything for his master.

A New 'Dream-Destroyer' To Overcome

However, trouble can start brewing even in the best of times. It wasn't long before Potiphar's wife wanted Joseph sexually. Over and over she cajoled him, "Come and lie with me."

But Joseph wasn't a fool. Each time Potiphar's wife propositioned him, he rejected her advances.

Now, this was a very wealthy and probably quite beautiful woman who wasn't accustomed to being rejected. She said, "Don't say no — come and lie with me, Joseph. My husband won't ever need to know. Come and lie with me."

Finally, one day when no one was in the house, she caught Joseph by his robe and commanded, *"Come on, Joseph, lie with me."*

But Joseph said to her, "No, I won't do that! Potiphar has made me the greatest one in all his house and has not kept one thing from me. I will not do this evil to him, nor will I do this evil to God" (Gen. 39:9). Then in his haste to leave the woman, Joseph left her still clutching his robe and ran out of the house.

Joseph made the determination, *"I will not do this evil in God's sight. I won't do it!"* Now, what would Joseph have said when Potiphar's wife disrobed in front of him if he'd had a victim's mentality? He would have said, "She belongs to me. She's mine. I've been taken advantage of long enough. I've been sold as a slave. I've been pushed around all these years. Potiphar owes me. God owes me. My brothers owe me. I've been waiting for the time when I could get something of Potiphar's. I've

28

been waiting for the time when I could get something from society. I deserve it, because *everyone owes me!*"

But instead of a *victim's* mentality, Joseph took on a *victor's* mentality.

When Potiphar's wife did this evil to Joseph, it took courage for him to run from her. David understood this kind of courageous decision. We see this in David's declaration in Psalm 101:3:

> **I will set nothing wicked before my eyes; I hate the work of those who fall away; it shall not cling to me.**

Joseph ran from Potiphar's wife because he was mindful of two things: 1) his relationship with God; and 2) his relationship with Potiphar. Joseph knew that giving into the woman's demands would have been wrong before God, and what God thought of the situation was ultimately all that mattered to Joseph.

Psalm 15:4 says that a righteous man "**...swears to his own hurt and does not change.**" Joseph was *not* going to change in order to accommodate someone else's flesh. *Joseph was a righteous man even when others around him were not righteous.* Even when he was victimized, even when people took advantage of him, Joseph always stayed the same.

You see, Joseph was always mindful of a truth that David later stated in Psalm 51:4: **"Against You, You only, have I sinned, and done this evil in Your sight...."** In other words, although Joseph understood that yielding to the demands of Potiphar's wife would have been a sin against Potiphar, he also realized it would have been an even greater sin against God. God was the One whom Joseph loved with all his heart. God is the One we are privileged to love as well.

Do you know what is so tragically funny about people who act like victims today? They walk around talking about how God instructed them to tell the world about their "victim-hood." They talk about how great it is with God.

"Praise the Lord, isn't it wonderful how God restored me?" they say. Yet at the same time, they expect others to take care of them for the rest of their lives.

This kind of behavior is wrong not only against man, but against God. That's why it's so important to understand what David understood in Psalm 51:4: **"Against You, You only, have I sinned, and done this evil in Your sight...."**

Joseph knew it was wrong to have sexual relations with Potiphar's wife, just as David knew it was wrong to have sexual relations with Uriah's wife, Bathsheba. That's why David said in Psalm 51, "What I did was wrong, God. And because it was wrong, I must be free from it. Lord, set me free from the wrong I committed against You."

Many years later, Jesus said something similar in Matthew 25:40:

"...Assuredly, I say to you, inasmuch as you did it to one of the least of these My brethren, you did it to Me."

Whenever we wrong another person, it is as if we have done it to God. This holds true:

● When we use our words in the wrong way.

● When we speak about other people in an incorrect manner.

- When we use another person as our "whipping boy," letting him bear the blame for our own wrongdoing.

When we blame someone else for the negative things going on in our lives, it is as if we have done it unto God.

Joseph was put in jail because of Potiphar's wife. The truth is, he probably just barely missed being stoned. According to the law of the time, taking someone else's wife was a very serious crime. The worst thing that happens today when this law is broken is that all the parties involved go on a television talk show to discuss their frustrations and the society that let them down!

But that wasn't the way it was in Joseph's time. He could have easily been stoned, beaten, or executed. But the Bible mentions no punishment other than being thrown in jail. That would have amounted to a slap on the wrist in Joseph's day!

That tells us something very interesting: *Potiphar didn't believe his own wife.* He believed Joseph. Potiphar knew which one would someday shatter his trust, and he knew which one would keep his word until death. But Potiphar had his reputation to maintain, so against his better judgment, he sided with his wife and threw Joseph in prison.

Driven by His Dream

As Joseph lay embarrassed and humiliated in a stinking, rat-infested Egyptian jail, his life seemed to lie in ruins. And even then he wasn't through being victimized. Later the king's cupbearer, whom Joseph helped by interpreting his dream, would forget about him and leave him to rot in jail after being released himself.

Yet still Joseph continued to rise to the top, even in prison. His God-given dream drove him on and gave him hope.

You see, Joseph was a driven man, *a man of destiny*. Throughout his life, it was the dream that kept driving Joseph on:

- It was the dream that kept him looking up from the pit of slavery.

- It was the dream that drove him to the head of Potiphar's household.

- It was the dream that gave him perspective when Potiphar's wife lied.

- It was the dream that helped him survive a damp, stinking, vile prison.

- It was the dream that helped him interpret Pharaoh's visions.

- It was the dream that finally made him the second most powerful man in the world!

So never underestimate the value of your dreams, and never deny yourself the chance to make those dreams come true.

Joseph never gave up. Before long, he rose to the top once again. He was soon running everything in jail. Time passed, and the Pharaoh had a dream. But when Pharaoh discussed his dream with his sorcerers and magicians, no one could interpret it.

That's when the cupbearer remembered the man in prison who had the gift of interpreting dreams. The cupbearer said to Pharaoh, "Your Majesty, I should have remembered this Hebrew earlier. This young man was in prison with me, and he interpreted my dream. In fact, O Pharaoh, that is the reason I stand before you this day."

At that moment, Joseph was brought out of prison. Through a series of remarkable events, he became the second greatest man in all of Egypt. When Joseph's chariot rolled down the street, everyone bowed in his presence — even nobles, generals, and the nation's top politicians!

Why was God able to cause this incredible turn-around of events? *Because Joseph never compromised; he never caved in nor yielded to unforgiveness and bitterness; and he never gave up on his dream.*

Remember, this was a *Hebrew*, a member of the most despised of races in the eyes of the Egyptians. Can you imagine what it was like for Joseph to go in one day from forced labor in prison on charges of raping his master's wife to being made the second most important man in the greatest nation of the world at that time?

Don't tell me that God won't change your circumstances! Joseph had every possible obstacle thrown at him in life, yet he became the second greatest man in all of Egypt.

Taking Steps Toward Forgiveness

Friend, when someone perpetrates a wrong against you, let Joseph be an example to you, and refuse to yield to bitterness. You need to understand these three words: *Time heals nothing!* Time doesn't heal wounds. When those wounds go unchecked, time simply makes those wounds worse. When you refuse to let go of hurts, you are fighting a battle you can never and will never win.

For instance, you may want to forgive someone from your church. But nothing will ever change if you stay on your side of the church and the other person stays on his side. Something more than time has to take place. You have to act. You have to move out and take a risk, just as Joseph did.

Some Christians never come face to face with real forgiveness because they won't deal with their hurts and offenses from their past. They just sit back and think that time will do the work.

If you want to take care of this problem the way Jesus instructed, you need to take the following two steps:

1. *Matthew 18:15* — When someone offends or sins against you, don't let it fester. Deal with it lovingly, kindly, and tactfully.

2. *Matthew 5:24* — Settle matters quickly. If someone is holding something against you, run toward that person, not away from him.

The apostle Paul said in Romans 12:21, **"Do not be overcome by evil, but overcome evil with good."** That's what you do when you face those who have abused you, offended you, or perpetrated evil against you!

Calling the Offender To Accountability

Most people live in their past, thinking about what someone has done against them but never confronting the offender with the truth. Sometimes so much time passes that the offended party can't even remember what the wrong was.

Friend, believe me when I say this to you: You can always find something to be offended about. People are talking about you when you don't even know it. Even your best friend may say something ugly about you once in a while.

So what do you do when you come face to face with your offender — with your "dream-destroyer"? The biblical response in that situation is the one that Joseph adopted.

Number one: Don't be afraid to confront others who have wronged you (Matt. 18:15). However, don't confront them with a hateful, argumentative spirit. Rather, deal with the situation in a spirit of love and compassion.

One of the greatest problems in our society today is that we don't make people personally responsible for anything. Kids shoot other kids in high school. Drug dealers operate in plain sight of our elementary schools. Murderers aren't accountable to their victims' families. Criminals get off with a slap on their wrists.

"It isn't their fault," sociologists tell us. "Those people were simply raised in a disadvantaged neighborhood or in an abusive family."

People are constantly doing wrong against other people, yet are not called into personal accountability for their actions. However, without accountability, the problem doesn't get fixed. Both the offender and the offended may go on in life assuming that everything is fine. But the truth is, everything is *not* fine.

When someone hurts or offends you and you don't confront the situation, frustrations and hurts can build and build and build on the inside of you until you finally explode. When that happens, you may stand there after

35

the explosion and have absolutely no idea why you are so hurt and upset. Why do you feel the way you do? Why are you so devastated? You just don't understand. Suddenly your entire life begins to be molded and shaped by wrong instead of right and by anger instead of love. You start being pushed around by your feelings.

Friend, if at this moment there is even one person you are holding something against — one person whom you wish you never had to see — you have a problem. If you have even one situation in your life that is emotionally tender, you have a problem. It's there, so stop pretending it isn't. It needs to be dealt with.

Joseph wasn't afraid to finally confront his brothers. These men had thrown Joseph into a pit and sold him into slavery, hoping that they would never see him again and that he would die a miserable death. *But Joseph knew God was in control, so he wasn't afraid to face those who had stolen his dreams.* We can see this is true as we compare what Joseph said to his brothers in Genesis 50 to Paul's words in Romans 8:

> **"But as for you, you meant evil against me; but God meant it for good, in order to bring it about as it is this day, to save many people alive."**
>
> **Genesis 50:20**

> **And we know that all things work together for good to those who love God, to those who are the called according to His purpose.**
>
> **Romans 8:28**

Don't Deny the Dream

What's the second thing you are to do when it's time to face the one who has wronged you? *Don't deny your shattered dream.*

Often people do their best to avoid the hurt and pain inflicted by "dream-destroyers." These people try to hide behind a façade of false piety and false spirituality, acting as if there is really no problem.

But Proverbs 13:12 says hope deferred makes the heart sick — and a problem denied causes hope to be deferred! For instance, someone with a runny nose, watery eyes, and "the sniffles" might put up a false front and claim, *"I'm not sick. I'm not sick!"* But believe me, denial is no substitute for real-life faith in God and His Word.

We know there is a right way to deal with sickness based on God's Word. When symptoms show up in our bodies (and even before we see the symptoms), we are to thank God that His Word is true. We thank Him that by the stripes of Jesus, we have been healed. We have been made whole. We have been made complete.

In the same way, before situations of offense ever arise, I am already thanking God for His Word. I am already saying what He says about my relationships with others.

The typical person will deny someone has hurt him. He will say, "I'm fine. I'm not hurt. I have no pain."

Although the Bible doesn't call this "denial," we know that psychologists use this term to describe the tendency to act as if pain doesn't exist. But no matter what that person says, the hurt is still there, and the only way for him to get over the pain is to deal with it according to God's Word. He must confront the offender and make him accountable for what he has done.

Paul even did this with Peter, the great apostle. In Galatians 2:11, Paul said, **"Now when Peter had come to Antioch, I withstood** [confronted] **him to his face, because he was to be blamed."** Peter was wrong, and his wrong affected many other people. Therefore, Paul found it necessary to confront Peter and call him to personal accountability for the wrong he had committed.

Godly Sorrow Leads to Repentance

The important thing is to right the wrong that has been done, not only in the eyes of men, but also in the eyes of God. Paul talks about this principle in Second Corinthians 7:8,9:

> **For even if I made you sorry with my letter, I do not regret it; though I did regret it. For I perceive that the same epistle made you sorry, though only for a while.**
> **Now I rejoice, not that you were made sorry, but that your sorrow led to repentance....**

When we come face to face with our offender in love and genuine honesty, our response to that person's offense can often shock him into waking up to God and His goodness.

Paul goes on to say in verse 9, **"...For you were made sorry in a godly manner, that you might suffer loss from us in nothing."** In other words, if you don't require personal responsibility — confronting what

38

people have done or perpetrated against you — those who have committed a wrong will suffer loss from you. In other words, they will be less than what God wants them to be if you don't confront them because you're afraid of what they may say. Whenever you avoid dealing with those who have offended you out of fear, they will suffer loss from you.

Then Paul says in verse 10, **"For godly sorrow produces repentance leading to salvation...."** The term "godly sorrow" comes from the Greek word *kadargodzumai*, meaning repentance that comes from the *inside* to the *outside*. This is when a person finally realizes what he has done wrong and says with a sincere heart, "Oh, God, I confess that I have sinned against You."

However, if the person's heart isn't right, he will say, "I'm the righteousness of God. I didn't do anything wrong!" Then he'll walk around with a rebellious, cocky attitude, completely devoid of godly sorrow.

A person who asks for blanket forgiveness is another example of someone devoid of godly sorrow. This kind of person says, "If I've ever done anything to hurt you, please forgive me."

When someone says that to me, I ask, "Well, what you have done?"

The answer will often come back, "I don't know, but if I ever did anything..."

I reply, "That means you are asking for forgiveness for something you never did."

"Well, yes, I guess that's true."

Do you know what psychologists call a person who does that? They call him a person with a "rescuer" complex, someone who is always trying to be a "savior" in difficult situations by taking the blame for something he didn't do.

But how can that person have godly sorrow over a situation that never happened? He can't, and only godly sorrow works repentance unto salvation. That's why Romans 12:18 says, **"If it is possible, AS MUCH AS DEPENDS ON YOU, live peaceably with all men."**

Take Personal Responsibility And Change Yourself

Now let's look at the third thing you should do when facing the one who has offended you: *You must take responsibility for your life and your attitude.* It is always appropriate to take responsibility for your own actions and then allow Jesus to become your "grief-bearer." In other words, you must allow Jesus to be the One who carries your sorrow and your pain. Then and only then will you find salvation working within you.

We are not to ignore hurts as if they never happened. Sure, we may have already said, "I forgive you" to the person who hurt us. But if we're really living in forgiveness, we shouldn't still be walking around with a chip on our shoulder. Perhaps it's time for us to get our attitude right and understand what forgiveness and repentance really mean!

The Bible says that godly sorrow works repentance unto salvation. That kind of repentance is genuine; it is *not* just a bunch of shallow proclamations. On the other hand, the sorrow of the world works death. That means people aren't operating in the right spirit when they continually come to you and say, "I'm really sorry for what I did. I feel so guilty. I don't know what to do about this. What I did was just horrible."

People like that don't want forgiveness; they simply want you to excuse their wrong behavior.

The person who is doing all that apologizing can't allow godly sorrow to work in him because he has fallen into the cheap sorrow of the world. The world says, "I'm sorry. There now — that should make everything okay again. You shouldn't have a problem with me anymore because I've said I'm sorry."

On the other hand, godly sorrow says, "Father, I take responsibility for my actions. First John 1:9 says, **'If we confess our sins, He is faithful and just to forgive us our sins and to cleanse us from all unrighteousness.'** So, God, not only do I lift this sin off me and give it to You, my sin-bearer, but I also realize that in my flesh dwells no good thing. I know that apart from You, my goodness is nothing." (*See* Psalm 16 and Romans 7.)

Yes, we are to call others to personal responsibility. However, there is also plenty of personal responsibility for us to accept as well. *We will never change anyone else until we change ourselves.*

As television host Jack Paar once said, "My life seems like one long obstacle course, with me as the chief obstacle." Author Norman Vincent Peale concurred with that sentiment when he said, "I'm the hardest person I've ever had to deal with."

Wife, do you want your husband to be more forgiving? *Be more forgiving toward him.*

Husband, do you want your wife to be more loving? *Work on being more loving toward her.*

41

Do you want your boss to be more understanding? *Try looking through his eyes, and then offer your understanding and compassion to him.*

Do you want your children to be more open with you? *Try being more open with them.*

Do you want to receive? *Learn how to give.*

You see, if a farmer wants to reap, he first has to sow. In the same way, if you want to receive anything in this life, you must first learn how to give.

It's true in every area of life. For instance, when you give your money at the store, you receive groceries in return. Before you give the money, you can look at the groceries and even hold them in your hands, but they can never be yours without the giving.

Jesus said it like this in Luke 6:36-38:

"Therefore be merciful, just as your Father also is merciful.
"Judge not, and you shall not be judged. Condemn not, and you shall not be condemned. Forgive, and you will be forgiven.
"Give, and it will be given to you: good measure, pressed down, shaken together, and running over will be put into your bosom. For with the same measure that you use, it will be measured back to you."

We are not to *react* to other people, circumstances, or events. We are to *act on God's Word.* We are to be "*act-ers,*" not "*react-ers.*" Simply put, *our real goal should be to learn how to live linked to God instead of chained to people and circumstances.* Part of this goal involves learning how to take personal responsibility for our own behavior.

That sense of personal responsibility causes us to act like Jesus did when He hung on the Cross and said, "Father, forgive them, for they know not what they do" (Luke 23:34). It causes us to act like Joseph when he said in Genesis 50:19, "Who am I to stand in the place of God?"

We must all stand before the Judgment Seat of Christ that we may be judged for the deeds we have done while in our earthly bodies, whether those deeds be good or bad. Therefore, I will not hold a person to what he has done against me. I will not make him be the sin-bearer. He is forgiven. I transfer the hurt and offense to a place in my walk with God that no man can touch, and I go on with my dream.

If I never bind others to the commitments they've made and the work they've done, they can never disappoint me nor control my destiny. After all, I never expect people to be what only God my Savior can be to me.

Nothing Can Stop Your Dream!

So remember, friend: *No man can stop your dream!* As someone once said, "If criticism had any real power to harm, the skunk would be extinct by now!"

No person, no circumstance, no setback, no carnal opinion — absolutely *nothing* can stop your dream if you refuse to let go of it. I like the way Winston Churchill put it when someone asked him to describe the most important lesson he had learned in life. Churchill shouted, *"Never give up; never give up; NEVER EVER GIVE UP!"*

The dream Joseph had in Genesis 37, before he was ever sold into slavery by his brothers, was the very dream that ultimately came to pass. Why did it come to

43

pass? *Because although Joseph held on to his dream, he never held on to a grudge.* He never nursed hatred in his heart, nor did he ever hold anyone to what they had done against him. Therefore, nothing was able to stop the dream God had given Joseph from coming to pass — and the same is true for you!

What To Do
When Your Dreams Seem Shattered

Joseph's story has touched my life in so many ways that it would be impossible to describe them all in one short book. That's why I think it's so important that you go back and study Joseph's life as you learn to overcome the criticism, abuse, and negligence of those who have hurt you and shattered your dreams.

As you study Joseph's life, I want you to remember eight important aspects of that story that literally changed the course of the Hebrew nation and, therefore, history itself.

1. JOSEPH WAS ABUSED.

Read Genesis 37 and see how Joseph was ridiculed, humiliated, and embarrassed by his own family. Has that ever happened to you? If it has, don't be deceived into thinking you're the only one who has ever been abused, neglected, or ridiculed. You just don't have the time to indulge in a pity party, for it could cost you your dream!

So whenever you get knocked down, don't just sit there; get up and keep moving! As John Mason says, *"Never surrender your dream to noisy negatives."*

2. JOSEPH'S OWN LOVED ONES PLOTTED AGAINST HIM.

Has anyone in the workplace ever undermined your effort? Has anyone at school or work tried to make you look bad in front of your teachers or supervisors? Don't give up just because of the smallness and shortcomings of those close to you. Keep your mind and heart focused on God's Word, and keep moving forward.

3. **EVEN THOUGH JOSEPH BECAME A SLAVE IN A HEATHEN COUNTRY, HE STOOD FIRM FOR GOD.**

Joseph never gave up nor shrunk back. He even accepted a position as an administrator in a country that hated his people in order to position himself for the fulfillment of his dream.

That's an important point to remember. Just like a football player has to keep himself in position to make the tackle, so we must be ready twenty-four hours a day for the opportunities God sets before us.

Have you shrunk back from Christian service? Have you decided not to take part in a secular job opportunity? Remember, you have been called to shine your light before men, not hide it under a bushel. So in spite of criticism, *stay in position for the fulfillment of your dream.* Don't move; don't give up; and don't shrink back!

4. **JOSEPH WAS CHALLENGED MORALLY, BUT HE WOULDN'T PAY THE DEVIL'S PRICE.**

One of Satan's most common strategies to get us sidetracked from our dreams is to tempt us toward moral failure. Adultery, affairs, pornography, and every other lust of the flesh are always waiting to destroy our dreams.

- A man's wife doesn't understand him, so he starts spending time with his secretary.

45

- A woman's husband seems uninterested, so she begins spending time with another man.

- Boredom sets in, so a person picks up that pornographic magazine.

The list goes on and on, and the consequences are severe. As my dear friend Peter Daniels has said, *"If you want to stop God's will, dreams, and destiny for your life, there is no quicker way to do it than with moral failure."*

Just think of the worldwide damage that the moral failures of a handful of men and women of God have caused in the last two decades. What is the bottom line? *Never put yourself in a position to make this kind of damaging mistake* (Psalm 101:3). Never compromise your strict standard of moral character — not even for one moment!

5. IN SPITE OF OVERCOMING ALL THOSE OBSTACLES, JOSEPH WAS LOCKED UP AGAIN.

At this point in the story, you might think that all was well with Joseph. You might assume that he was on his way to achieving great success. But, sadly, after Joseph did the right thing by refusing to have an affair with Potiphar's wife, he still ended up in jail!

So don't think that once you get back on track with God, life will be a sweet success story. Difficult times *will* come; critics will still be out there. Nevertheless, you must go on in the power of the Holy Spirit.

I'm reminded of the church in Kansas City whose slogan is as follows: *Wake up, sing up, preach up, pray up, and pay up — but never give up, let up, back up, or shut up until the cause of Christ in this church and in the world is built up!*

6. JOSEPH DIDN'T GET MAD AT GOD; HE GOT BACK IN THE SYSTEM.

Looking back, I don't think I've ever met a successful man or woman who attributed any of his or her failures to God. Joseph certainly didn't. Even though he was tossed right back into cruel bondage, he never once yelled at God or tried to get even.

Because Joseph maintained a right attitude of heart, God granted him favor in the eyes of the warden. In fact, Joseph was made administrator of that stinking pit not long after he was thrown into prison. *Once again, he was continuing to position himself for the fulfillment of his dream.*

7. EVERY MAN OR WOMAN HAS HIS OR HER HOUR.

God never forgets our circumstances or leaves us behind. We may not understand His timing. But as long as we stand on His Word and believe His promises, He will always be faithful to give us our chance. He really is *the God of a second chance* — or the third or fourth or fifth or sixth chance!

8. FINALLY, AFTER THIRTEEN LONG YEARS, JOSEPH'S DREAM WAS RESTORED.

Joseph refused to live out of his woundedness. He learned to forgive his brothers and let it go, because real love doesn't take into account a wrong suffered.

When God restored Joseph's dream, it was awesome indeed. Second only to Pharaoh, Joseph was the lord of all he surveyed. He had all the money, respect, and resources of the civilized world at his feet.

As we read on into the book of Exodus, it's interesting to note that after Joseph's death, the Hebrew oppression

47

soon began. Why? Because Joseph's mighty presence in Egypt was the only thing that kept the hand of bondage off the shoulders of the Hebrew people.

God used Joseph to protect His people. The Hebrews' awful oppression began because no one was left in power who would defend them.

How's that for a lesson in positioning ourselves for the fulfillment of our dream?

Peter Daniels says *you must simply want to change your generation.* So don't waste your time wondering what role you could possibly have in achieving such a lofty goal. How do you know that God isn't grooming you for a key position in advancing the Kingdom of God on this earth — protecting the Church and reaching the lost?

Don't Quit Until God Has Finished Your Story!

Don't give up; don't cash in; don't surrender. God isn't through with you — He's only beginning. Through handicaps, defeats, and struggles, God is still in control, and your destiny is yet to be determined.

Speaking of determination, let me ask you this question: *When a man is determined, what can stop him?*

- Cripple him, and you have Sir Walter Scott.

- Put him in prison, and you have John Bunyan.

- Bury him in the snows of Valley Forge, and you have George Washington.

- Cause him to be born in abject poverty, and you have Abraham Lincoln.

- Afflict him with asthma, and you have Theodore Roosevelt.

- Put him in the grease pit of an automotive garage, and you have Walter Chrysler.

- Make him second fiddle in an obscure American orchestra, and you have Toscanini.

- Afflict him with tuberculosis until he coughs up enough blood to cover his bedroom walls, and you have Oral Roberts.

- Burn him with napalm until even his family can't recognize him, and you have evangelist Dave Roever.

- Give him a mother who tries to abort him five times and causes him to be an illiterate, and you have a Peter Daniels.

- Lock him in a mental hospital and take away all hope for the future — and you have me, Robb Thompson.

That's why I'm telling you, friend — *don't quit until God has finished your story!*

I urge you to pray this short prayer right now. Let this be the moment that you let go of all those negative feelings that hold you back from seeing your dreams restored:

Father, first I thank You for Your Word, because the promises that You made to men like Joseph are the same promises I can stand on today. You are a God who never changes; there-fore, I can call on those promises to deliver me from the problems, difficulties, and struggles I face in my own life.

Second, I release the anger, bitterness, and hatred that I feel about my situation. I give it all to You. I also give You all my fear and apprehen-sion.

Third, I ask You to stand with me as I prayer-fully and graciously confront those who have wronged me. Help me speak with them not in anger or fear, but in the liberating power of Your Spirit, knowing that as I forgive them, You forgive me.

Finally, I pray that the dream You placed in my heart will once again burn with the fire and direction of Your Spirit. I pray that every hope, goal, and aspiration will be fulfilled as I put You first in my life and step out to a new level of faith. In the name of Your Son Jesus, amen.

Remember, friend — *you are a courageous achiever with dreams to light your way.*

ACTION POINTS FOR RESTORING YOUR DREAM

- Don't be afraid to confront others who have wronged you.

- Don't deny your shattered dream.

- Take responsibility for your actions.

- Realize that you will never change anyone else until you change yourself.

- Recognize that no man can stop your dream!

Chapter 2

SECURING YOUR DREAM:

Overcoming Stumbling Blocks to Success

O vercoming the pain and disappointment caused by shattered dreams is a long and often difficult process. But once it's accomplished, it will change your life forever.

Over the years as I have preached the Gospel, I've discovered that people frequently continue to stumble over the same mistakes and errors over and over again. Throughout their lives, even though they try to live for God, they continue to sin, experience hurt and pain, and fall short of the successful and abundant life God has provided for them.

In this chapter, I want to outline some principles that I believe are critical for success in our Christian walk. After all, the devil is very real, and his greatest goal is to distract us from God's promises and His grace. Therefore, it's imperative that we keep our eyes on the goal and live in the constant grace and protection of our Lord Jesus Christ.

Originally, I hadn't planned on including this chapter. But after much study and many conversations with people who have experienced the pain of shattered dreams, I decided it was important to give you a solid basis for continuing on with your life after your dreams are restored. After all, having dreams is one thing; keeping them alive with the fire of the Holy Spirit is quite another!

I'll tell you up front that I'm not going to pull any punches or soften any blows in this chapter. I've taken much of its material directly from my sermon transcripts and teachings in hopes that its frank, unadorned approach will speak to you on a gut level.

God's Word is an uncompromising, unflinching standard by which we must pattern our lives. Therefore, I'm going to tell it like it is and pray that God will use this discussion to help you break through the difficulties you're experiencing.

Removing the Negative Things From Your Life

To successfully continue your Christian walk after your dream has been restored, you need to apply the following guidelines to your life.

Number one: Remove negativity from your life. One of the most important truths I've learned over the years is this: *The only reason we fail is that we allow negative habits, relationships, attitudes, and so forth, to remain in our lives. In other words, we fail to maintain focus.* If we were to take out all these negative things, all that would be left is success.

Look at your life closely. What have you allowed to stay in your life that isn't directly in line with God's Word? Is there a constant, nagging sin you need to lay at

54

the Cross? Do you have a hidden poor attitude that is waiting to be dealt with?

Check to see what negative things need to be removed from your life. These things may not cost you your salvation, but they will act as stumbling blocks, preventing you from living truly a successful and fulfilling life.

- Perhaps you're still sneaking a look at pornographic magazines.

- Perhaps you still yield to that nagging desire to talk about people behind their backs.

- Perhaps you still don't quite tell the truth on your income tax.

- Perhaps it's just too easy to roll over and sleep on Sunday morning instead of getting your family to church.

Look at the negative things that still plague your life, and then root them out. Make a determined effort to live your life transparently before the Lord. Do everything honestly and with integrity as unto Him.

In this age of permissiveness, "doing your own thing" has almost become a religion. It's high time we got back to the basics and learned the true meaning of self-discipline! How do we start? By taking the time to examine our lives and root out everything that doesn't line up with God's Word.

Number two: Recognize that success is more than financial wealth. Too often, people equate success with financial gain. But frankly, that is only one of the many aspects of real success. Actually, I believe a person must succeed on the *inside* first before he can really handle and enjoy financial blessings on the *outside.*

In Joseph's case, his identity wasn't found in what he possessed materially; rather, it was found in his relationship with God.

I'm sure you've heard stories about people who were successful according to the world's standards but still spent a lot of time at the therapist's office. Simply put — they were successful on the outside, but inside they were terrible failures.

Take a look at Psalm 30:11,12:

> **You have turned for me my mourning into dancing; you have put off my sackcloth and clothed me with gladness,**
> **To the end that my glory may sing praise to You and not be silent. O Lord my God, I will give thanks to You forever.**

The psalmist was saying, "You have turned my sadness into joy. You have turned my misery into gladness. You have changed me from *within*, not just from without."

Even many Christians have the idea that more success translates as "more money." One of the great misinterpretations of the prosperity movement is that to be a successful believer, a person has to make a lot of money. But that couldn't be further from the truth.

Of course God cares about our finances. Of course He wants us to be more than able to pay our bills. Of course there are divine laws of giving and receiving. But God never intended for us to focus our energy and attention on making more money. Successful living means becoming successful in all areas of life — in our marriages, with our children, on our jobs, in our churches, etc. There's just so much more to living successfully than attaining financial wealth.

Many people also have the mistaken idea that money will solve all their problems. Friend, don't make that same mistake. The truth is, you'll deal with more problems when you have more money than you ever did when you were broke. You'll also face many more opportunities for failure after you've achieved financial success than you ever did before.

Remember, possessing a great deal of money means taking on a great deal of responsibility. A prosperous lifestyle doesn't just include new homes, new cars, and trips to the Rivera. It is also involves feeding the poor, educating disadvantaged children, reaching the lost, and supporting the Church.

Make Sure You're Successful On the Inside First

Number three: You must succeed on the INSIDE before you can succeed on the OUTSIDE. The violation of this principle was the main reason the American welfare system was in such desperate need of reform a few years ago. The government never required anything of anyone in order for them to receive financial help. As a result, many people had no desire to change their circumstances. They never even tried to change the way they thought, the way they acted, or how they conducted their lives. They had no need to change. After all, the money was available; all they had to do is reach out for it.

But I like what the Holy Spirit said through the apostle Paul in Second Thessalonians 3:10: **"...If anyone will not work, neither shall he eat."**

Hunger is a great motivator. Now, please understand my meaning here. I probably have more respect for a person who robs a bank than I do for a person who spends his or her life on welfare.

You may say, "Well, wait a minute, Robb. One of those activities is illegal, and the other is legal." That's true, and I would never advocate anyone breaking the law. But the man who perpetually lives on welfare takes something for nothing his entire life. He has no desire to ever change. He has no desire to get ahead in life and to do what it takes to succeed.

Perhaps you are on welfare right now. However, the very fact you are reading this book is an indication to me that you don't want to spend the rest of your life receiving handouts.

Actually, that is why the welfare system was instituted in this country in the first place. It was never meant to support a person forever. The purpose of welfare is to help a person in the short term while he is in the early stages of his journey to success.

You know, we live in a great country. We want to help people get up when they're down so they can begin to make a success of their lives. We are the only country that has what is called "a basement level" of poverty.

Our basement level of poverty right now is approximately $14,000 to $15,000 per year. If you don't make at least $14,000 per year, the government considers you impoverished. So we as a country give you something because we want to bless you. We want to help you get up and improve your life. No matter where you are today financially, we don't want you to be forced to remain at that level.

This is a continuous cycle in life. The truth is, I don't like where I am today either. I am in the deepest poverty I'll ever be in my life. This is the most impoverished I ever hope to be. This is also the worst health I ever hope to be in.

I am on my way up. I'm not staying where I am. I'm continually moving on, praise God. I'm growing. I'm going to do what God has called me to do. I will claw my way to that goal until I reach it. I am not going to lose in the game of life. I refuse to lose because I only get to play this game one time.

Now, let's talk about the person who robs a bank for a moment. That person is using man's ideas and the devil's methods. His method is wrong, but his desire (to have money) is right.

Your desire to have money is a good desire; just don't use the wrong method to fulfill it. The bank robber probably thought, *I know if I just had this money, all my problems would be over.* But as I said before, your problems aren't over when you have money — they're multiplied! That's why it's so important to make sure you stay on *God's* path to financial increase. Focus on becoming successful on the inside while you allow God to prosper you according to His Word.

In the process of making my own dreams come true, I discovered this principle of becoming successful on the inside first. At times, I found it necessary to let go of certain desires that seemed legitimate in themselves. In fact, I learned that if I didn't feel right about things *inside*, I shouldn't even make a move.

Let me give you an illustration. Some time ago, I bought a new car. When I first went to the car dealer, he offered me to sell me a better car, sticker-priced at $20,000 more than the car I intended to buy, for the same price as the less expensive car.

Now, most people would say, "Of course you should buy the better car, Robb! Man, oh, man! Isn't God blessing you! Look at how He's taking care of you!"

I test drove the more expensive car for a day and then gave it right back. You see, I knew I had yet to achieve that level on the inside, and where I was on the inside mattered to me more than money did. So I paid exactly the same amount of money for a car worth $20,000 less, and I've never regretted it.

The same is true for you. It's where you are on the inside that matters, not what car you drive or what clothes you wear. Just because you can afford something means very little. Big deal. Drug dealers can afford expensive things too! So what if you can afford it? Are you happy on the inside? Can you see yourself living at that level? Can you see yourself driving that car? Can you see yourself wearing those clothes?

Joseph's life rose only to the level he had attained on the inside.

In my own experience, I found that as I became more interested in the success of God's Kingdom and my own walk with God and less interested in my external success, new doors of opportunity began to open to me everywhere.

In the same way, friend, if you have a dream in your heart that is in line with God's Word, and if you focus on becoming all you should be on the inside, it will only be a matter of time before you see the fulfillment of that God-given dream.

Know Who You Are in Christ

Number four: Success is not an outward manifestation of AFFLUENCE; it is an inward manifestation of INFLUENCE. Joseph never forgot who he was and to whom he belonged.

As the devil turns up the heat on this world, we are finding out who the true believers are and who they are not. We see Christians shouting on Sunday and doubting on Monday. Why does this happen? Because these people have lost sight of their identities as believers.

You know, when I was a child, a person might not attend church or believe in God, but at least he respected those who did. Even up to the end of the 1970s and the beginning of the 1980s, it was still almost fashionable to be a Christian. But it isn't like that in today's society. The situation has really changed. There are even people who would kill a Christian and think they were doing God a favor! Why has this change occurred? *Because most Christians have let the world and not God dictate who they are.*

Many Christians have gotten drunk on the spirit of the world rather than on the Spirit of God. Meanwhile, the devil has been turning up the heat in the world. As Jesus said in John 10:10: **"The thief does not come except to steal, and to kill, and to destroy...."**

The devil isn't making anyone rich. The devil comes only to steal, kill, and destroy. But whenever the enemy turns up the heat, the Spirit of God always raises up a standard against him.

You see, Jesus came to earth for one purpose, which is also stated in John 10:10: **"...I have come that they may have life, and that they may have it more abundantly."** I like to say it this way: *"I am come that you would have life, superabundant in quantity and superior in quality."*

How would you like to live a life that is *superabundant in quantity* and *superior in quality*? Well, the first step is to discover and then live according to who you are in Christ.

How does God look at you personally? In His eyes, you are destined for greatness, for He has designed you to succeed. You have within you the motivating factor for success because you know on the inside that you want to make it. You don't have the will to die; you have the will to *live*. And you don't want to just barely get by — you want to live life to its fullest!

As Christians, we are not destined to lose. Jesus made us winners. And if Jesus has already made you and me winners, then, bless God, we're going to do what it takes to win!

Suppose someone you trusted came to you and said, "There is a million dollars down at the end of the block. It's for you, but you have to go get it. On your way, someone is going to tell you the money really isn't for you, but don't believe him. Just go to the end of the block to pick up your prize, and don't believe anyone who discourages you along the way."

Well, that is a good picture of the way it is with you and God. The prize is already at the end of your believing. It's already there, waiting for you to enjoy it on this side of Heaven. But every day a voice tells you that the prize isn't real; that the prize is for someone else, not for you; or that no one is actually getting the prize.

Understand this, friend: That voice is lying to you.

We can see what God wants to do for you by taking a look at Psalm 20:4:

> **May He grant you according to your heart's desire, and fulfill all your purpose.**

God wants to fulfill *all* your purpose. That's talking about all the dreams He has placed in your heart. God wants to fulfill those dreams and cause them to be manifested in your life.

Second Corinthians 1:20 says, **"For all the promises of God in Him are Yes...."** Notice that it doesn't say, "All the promises of God are *sometimes* — sometimes He says *yes*; sometimes He say *maybe*; and sometimes He says *wait.*"

No, it doesn't say that. Paul said, **"For all the promises of God in Him are *Yes.*"** They are *yes*! Sadly, most Christians are still trying to decide if God really meant what He said.

Did you know that many Christians live and die without ever seeing their dreams fulfilled? Often these same Christians spend all their time being concerned about whether or not other people view them as a success. People who do that are missing a vital key to securing their dreams: They have to learn to view *themselves* as a success — understanding who they are in light of God's Word and never believing for a moment what anyone else thinks to the contrary.

Who are you? You can't be like a spiritual chameleon, changing identities the way a chameleon changes colors.

You know what people want you to say, so that's what you say. You know how people want you to act, so that's how you act. You know what it will take to succeed in your company, so that's exactly what you do. But in the process of conforming to what other people want, you become untrue or unfaithful to everything you are. And by becoming unfaithful to yourself, you eventually forget who you really are.

Don't let this happen to you. *You have to maintain your identity according to God's Word.*

This is where I veer from the canned, "garden-variety" success teaching. Most success teachers tell you to believe in yourself, not in someone else. But the question you *should* be asking yourself is "What does *God* think about me?"

So who does God say you are? For one thing, He identifies you as part of His family. Look at what Paul says in Galatians 2:20 about your identity as a child of God:

"I have been crucified with Christ; it is no longer I who live, but Christ lives in me; and the life which I now live in the flesh I live by faith in the Son of God, who loved me and gave Himself for me."

I'm reminded of John the Baptist. Here was a man who lived in the wilderness, a man whom multitudes of people came to see on a daily basis. The Pharisees and Sadducees were curious about this man, so they questioned John the Baptist regarding his true identity. They asked him, "Are you the Christ?"

"I am not," John replied.

They questioned again: "Then are you Elijah?"

"No, I am not Elijah either."

"Well, then, *you* tell *us*. Who are you?"

John responded, *"I am a voice."* (A voice has no face, no personal identity.)

"I am the voice of one crying in the wilderness."

The people went out in the wilderness to be baptized by John. Leaving behind their old identities, they picked up new identities with God.

John's attitude about his own identity is nowhere more evident than when his disciples reported to him that more people were getting baptized by Jesus' disciples than by him.

Now, what would most people do if they heard that someone else was taking over the spotlight they had once enjoyed? What would they do if they heard someone else was being preferred over themselves? I'll tell you what they'd do: They'd begin to talk negatively about their rival in order to make themselves look good!

But John the Baptist didn't do that. Instead, he said, "Jesus must increase, and I must decrease. Nothing has been given to any man except what has been given to him from Heaven [John 3:27,30]." In other words, John was saying, *"It's okay; I'm just the voice. My true identity rests in the One who must increase, even as I must decrease."* As a result, Jesus' words came to pass in John's life: "He who does the truth comes to the light, and it will be made manifest that his deeds are of God [v. 21]."

In the same way, we must lose our natural identity and pick up Christ's voice within us. We pick up our identity in the Creator of the universe, even though we ourselves are not the creator. As Jesus said in John 15:5:

"I am the vine, you are the branches. He who abides in Me, and I in him, bears much fruit; for without Me you can do nothing."

You can do absolutely nothing without Jesus. You are only a voice; you are not an independent personality. You don't possess anything on your own. Your success is not linked to who you are or who you are not, nor to what you feel or think about anything. Rather, it is completely linked to what Jesus said and who He is.

You can see why it's so important to *know who you are in Christ*!

Be Willing To Bear Pain

Number five: Recognize that success is the willingness to bear pain. Joseph willingly bore the hardship of resisting temptation. His hardship was outwardly imposed by others, but his commitment to God was self-imposed.

My friend Peter Daniels once gave an unusual definition for success. He said, *"Success is the willingness to bear pain."* When I first heard that, I thought, *Gosh, Peter, you've really missed it.* I doubted his statement for two reasons.

First, I always test everything in light of the Word of God. My first response was that Peter's statement didn't line up with the Word.

I have to find everything in the Scriptures, or I can't believe it. You see, God's Word is the most important thing in my life. Nothing is more important to me. I enjoy it. I spend time in it. As a matter of fact, I want God's Word more than I want to breathe because I know I can get breath with God's Word, but I can't get God's Word with breath. In other words, my natural life cannot produce my spiritual life, but my spiritual life can produce a good natural life.

Second, I used to think of success the way most people do — related to joy, happiness, and the easy life, which is the exact opposite of "pain."

I started thinking about the connection between pain and success, so of course I went straight to the Bible. I wondered, *What does God's Word say about the willingness to bear pain?*

I remembered Roman 8:17, which says if I am a child of God, I am also an heir of God and a joint heir with Christ. Paul goes on to say that if I suffer with Jesus, I will also be glorified with Him.

Then I thought, *Wait a second. If I am a child, then I am an heir of God and joint heir with Christ. But why didn't Paul end the verse there?*

I'll tell you why the verse didn't end there: *Because pain comes with winning.* Ask any Olympic champion. There is pain in training. There is a cost to winning — a cost that losers never pay.

But notice that Paul says we suffer *with* Christ. At least we're not suffering *without* Him! Jesus is right there beside us, going through exactly what we're experiencing.

Consider the rich young ruler, who came to Jesus and asked, **"...Good Master, what shall I do to inherit eternal life?"** (Luke 18:18 *KJV*). That young man didn't realize that there was nothing he could do in his limited situation to inherit eternal life.

Jesus gently explained to the rich young ruler that it is harder for a camel to go through the eye of a needle than it is for a rich man to enter into the Kingdom of God. Then He said, **"...How hard it is for those who have riches to enter the kingdom of God!"** (v. 24).

Look at what First Timothy 6:17 says:

Command those who are rich in this present age not to be haughty, nor to trust in uncertain riches but in the living God, who gives us richly all things to enjoy.

God gives you good things so you can enjoy them. He wants you to enjoy your success and what He has called you to do in life.

Honestly, none of us want the hard parts of life; none of us want the obstacles. All of us want the prize that is on the other side of the obstacle. But there is something we have to go through to get to the other side, and that something is *pain*.

I like what Jesus said in Mark 10:29,30:

"...Assuredly, I say to you, there is no one who has left house or brothers or sisters or father or mother or wife or children or lands, for My sake and the gospel's,
"who shall not receive a hundredfold now in this time — houses and brothers and sisters and mothers and children and lands, with persecutions — and in the age to come, eternal life."

Now, *why* did Jesus have to put in those two words "with persecution"? Why can't we just have success *without* persecution for a change? Why can't we ever win in life without the devil fighting us every step of the way?

We can learn a lesson from the apostle Paul, who explained why *he* continually faced opposition in his life and ministry:

...Lest I should be exalted above measure by the abundance of the revelations....

2 Corinthians 12:7

Let me give you the "Robb Thompson" version of Paul's words in verses 7 and 8: "There was given unto me a thorn in the flesh, the messenger of Satan, to buffet me, to beat me on the ears, to 'whap' me all over the street, lest I should be exalted above measure. I sought the Lord three different times about this 'thorn,' begging Him to make it depart from me. But I had something to learn: I had to find out that God's grace is sufficient for me, even in the midst of pain."

We've all prayed at one time or another, "God, take this out of my life! Please, God, take this out of my life!" But remember, success is the willingness to bear pain. We can only find success when we learn how to take the persecutions we face and turn them around for good. But it's up to us to use the hard times we go through as seeds of greatness instead of seeds of defeat, as the prelude to winning instead of to losing.

You see, ultimately no one can destroy your dream but you. So learn from the pain you encounter in life, and someday you will reach the level the original disciples achieved. They were persecuted, hunted down like animals, beaten, whipped, and murdered in the most horrible and unthinkable ways. Yet they never gave in, nor did they ever quit — and today they are sitting in heavenly places with Jesus, celebrating eternity!

So I guess Peter Daniels was right after all. Success *is* the willingness to bear pain!

Success Is Never Achieved Alone

Number six: Understand that no one is a success alone. Promotion comes from God through the hand of someone else. Joseph understood this principle.

Success cannot be linked to you alone. Whatever success you hope to enjoy in life must be linked to the people you touch in some tangible way. Success is more than benefits you alone will receive. Your success must have within it the seeds that will produce much fruit. All of mankind should be able to eat of the fruit of your tree of success. But fruit only results when you have withstood pain. By overcoming rejection, inner turmoil, and outer failure time after time, you finally come to a place of success.

Personally, I continually meditate on what success really is. I've come up with a definition of success I believe you will enjoy. It's one that I am constantly expanding on.

To me, success can be defined as follows: *The divine providence of God opening His documents on the emancipation of mankind in order to give me the ability to explore, examine, define, understand, enjoy, fulfill, and bring to pass the depths of His grace to my entire generation.*

I have made up my mind to win, even if it changes the way I live. I *will* win because I refuse to take no as an answer. I am not going to stay the way I am right now. I am going to win in the game of life as no one has ever won. That is my choice, and that should be your choice as well.

As for me, I recognize that I cannot be a success independently of all others. Nevertheless, I *can* and I *do* choose my destiny: *God's dream in me fulfilled to the utmost!*

The Value of Servanthood

Number seven: Learn to become a servant. Joseph never lost his position of servanthood. In spite of his ups and downs, he never lost his desire to serve. In fact, after he was put in charge of all of Egypt, his greatest concern was to take care of his family.

The best thing you and I could ever be called is a servant. I consider the title "Servant" to be the greatest title I'll ever bear. A servant is no longer interested in his own success; rather, he is willing to get involved in the vision of another.

Personally, I am only interested in the success God gives to me as a believer and a joint heir with Jesus. I'm not interested in what I can do on my own. I'm only interested in what God has said about me and whom He has made me in Christ.

Why is this perspective so important? Because it takes the pressure off us. When we become concerned about the things of God, we take our focus off our problems, our difficulties, and our struggles. Suddenly we discover the enormous potential that is ours in Jesus.

I highly recommend that you read the classic book by Dale Carnegie called *How To Win Friends and Influence People.* Although it isn't written from the perspective of God's Word, it will give you some wonderful techniques and insights into serving other people and learning how to concentrate on others instead of yourself.

All great salesmen understand that you'll never get anywhere until you genuinely help the customer solve his problem. Helping other people solve their difficulties is the greatest single way to solve your own problems. This is true with your friends, your family, and anyone else you come in contact with.

Get your focus off yourself, and pour your interest and concern into other people. Become a servant!

Abide in God's Word

Number eight: Stay in God's Word. God emphasizes this all-important principle in Joshua 1:8:

> **"This Book of the Law shall not depart from your mouth, but you shall meditate in it day and night, that you may observe to do according to all that is written in it. For then you will make your way prosperous, and then you will have good success."**

God says here that abiding in the Word is the way to make your way prosperous. So according to this verse, is it wrong to possess wealth? No, but don't go after money at the expense of enjoying your life. Stay in the Word, and let God prosper you. Don't work so hard at becoming rich. Learn a lesson from those who have desperately pursued becoming rich, only to fall into temptations and snares along the way. Remember Paul's warning in First Timothy 6:9,10:

> **But those who desire to be rich fall into temptation and a snare, and into many foolish and harmful lusts which drown men in destruction and perdition.**
> **For the love of money is a root of all kinds of evil, for which some have strayed from the faith in their greediness, and pierced themselves through with many sorrows.**

All that you are and all that you have can be attributed to what Jesus has done through you. Therefore, you have to come to a place in life where you're excited about where Jesus lets you live, what He lets you drive, and how much money you have in your pocket.

Work on becoming successful on the inside instead of killing yourself for money. Set your focus on the One who made you who you are, and He will prosper you in all that you do.

You may be thinking, *Man, oh, man! God is going to help me become prosperous and live on "easy street"!*

But living in abundance and prosperity doesn't come cheap. There are always obstacles to overcome when you set out to succeed in life. Mark 11:23 talks about those obstacles:

> **"For assuredly, I say to you, whoever says to this mountain** [the mountain represents a problem], **'Be removed** [removal represents the answer] **and be cast into the sea,' and does not doubt in his heart** [doubt represents another problem]...."

Where did that doubt come from? The doubt came from your past. It came from last week, last month, last year. One place doubt *didn't* come from, however, is the Word of God. That's why you will never be the same when you learn to live your life through the filter of God's Word.

Quit Blame-Shifting

Number nine: Stop blaming others. One of the most important faults to overcome in making your dreams a reality is the tendency to blame others for your problems.

Blaming someone else started in the Garden of Eden. God put His human creations in the Garden and then walked with them in the cool of the day. Later the serpent came and deceived Eve into eating the forbidden fruit. Eve then gave the fruit to her husband, who also ate of it. Afterward, God came walking in the Garden, looking for His friends.

"Hey, where are you two?" God called. "Adam, where are you?"

In great fear, Adam replied, "I'm right here behind this tree. I didn't want You to see me because I'm naked."

"Who told you that you were naked?" God asked. "Did you eat of the fruit of the tree in the midst of the Garden, the one I warned you about?"

Adam responded, "It was the woman You gave me! She gave me the fruit, and I ate it."

Then God turned to Eve and asked, "What is this you have done?"

Eve replied, "It was the serpent's fault! He deceived me!"

Notice that the blame for Adam and Eve's sin was ultimately laid on the devil, not on Adam or Eve. God said to the serpent, *"Now you are cursed above all."*

But even today, mankind still has to live with the consequences of that sin. The fact is that nearly every day, we all have a desire to blame others for our problems.

Husbands blame their wives: "You're always picking a fight with me. It's your fault."

Wives blame their husbands: "You never love me the way you're supposed to. You always judge me. It's *your* fault."

Brothers and sisters are often pros at blaming each other: "I didn't do it — *she* did it! It's *her* fault!"

At this point, let me say that you should never let your children fight with each other. How do you keep them from doing this? Let me put it in scriptural terms:

Do not withhold discipline from a child; if you punish him with the rod, he will not die.

Proverbs 23:13 *NIV*

Discipline your son, for in that there is hope; do not be a willing party to his death.

Proverbs 19:18 *NIV*

When you let children fight with each other, they "bite and devour one another" (Gal. 5:15) and eventually risk killing each other inside. So never let your children fight with or judge each other. Don't let them pass off their own responsibility by blaming their brother or sister for what *they* did wrong.

Also, if you are an employee, make sure you don't always blame your employer for the things that go wrong on the job.

A friend once told me, "My boss doesn't know anything."

I said, "I know; that's why he hired you — to solve his problems for him! Why don't you pray for him?"

"Pray for him!" my friend exclaimed.

75

"In fact, why don't you pray for your supervisor to get a promotion?" I asked. My friend didn't know *what* to do with that suggestion!

I used to get rid of more supervisors that way. My supervisor would say to me, 'Thompson, I'm going to bury you in work."

I'd just look at him and reply, "Sir, with all due respect, you don't have enough work to bury me. And by the way, Sir, I just want to let you know that I'm going to work hard to make sure you get a promotion."

Later when my supervisors received a promotion, they'd come back to me and ask, "How did you know that was going to happen?"

"I have friends in high places!" I'd reply.

Don't Waste Time Blaming Yourself

Number ten: Stop blaming yourself. The act of blaming yourself is one of the most self-destructive tendencies of our society. Wives frequently go to talk to a counselor and say, "I know it's my fault, not his fault." I also hear people say, "I'm so stupid. I don't know why I keep making mistakes like that. I never seem to do the right thing. I'm always doing the wrong thing."

Does that sound familiar?

When you blame yourself, that frees you from the responsibility of fixing the problem. That's why you will never grow until you get past the point of blaming yourself and begin to forgive yourself.

Second Corinthians 5:21 says, **"For He made Him who knew no sin to be sin for us, that we might become the righteousness of God in Him."** Colossians 1:22 explains this concept further, saying that God has reconciled us to Himself by the sacrifice of Christ's earthly body through death in order to present us holy, unblameable, unaccusable, and unreproveable, without fault or failure in our Father's sight.

You may say, "I could really get things done if I were just righteous." But, friend, if you are a child of God, you are already righteous. The Bible says you've already won. The reason you are miserable is that you are not living out who you really are in Christ!

We've looked at ten guidelines you can follow to secure your dream after God has restored it to new life in your heart. As you are faithful to follow these guidelines, you will get yourself in position for that dream to finally be fulfilled — in real time, on this side of Heaven!

ACTION POINTS FOR SECURING YOUR DREAM

- Remove the negative things from your life.

- Remember that success is more than financial wealth.

- Recognize that you must succeed on the inside before you can succeed on the outside.

- Understand that success isn't an outward manifestation of *affluence*; it is an inward manifestation of *influence*.

- Don't forget that success is the willingness to bear pain.

- Recognize that no one is a success alone.

- Learn to become a servant.

- Stay in God's Word.

- Stop blaming others.

- Stop blaming yourself.

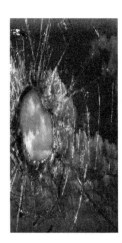

Chapter 3

Realizing Your Dream:

Finding Success In the Workplace

Your dreams often have a strong relationship to your job or career. Therefore, I want to close this book with a special chapter that explains how you can maintain your dreams in the high-pressure world of the workplace.

Contrary to what most people think, the Bible has always had a great deal to say about our work. For instance, when the people of Israel began to build a great temple for the worship of God, skilled craftsmen were celebrated and honored. Throughout the Old Testament, you can see the importance of carpenters, laborers, designers, artists, and other workers of all kinds.

In the New Testament, many of the disciples were fishermen, and Jesus met them right at the point of their work. Notice how many of the stories and parables Jesus related had to do with fish and fishing. Other parables had to do with farming and other forms of labor. In fact, planting and harvesting are important concepts used throughout the Scriptures. And don't forget the tent-making ministry of the apostle Paul!

This is a good place to point out that, in my estimation, one of the most important jobs in the world is that of *housewife and mother*. In today's society, mothers often get the short end of the stick, so to speak. But I believe that in God's order of things, the mother's role in creating a solid home environment and raising up her children in the ways of God is both important and precious. So if you're a mother reading this book, I highly encourage you to apply the following principles to your work in the home.

I want to talk about two aspects of the Bible that have always stood out to me:

The Bible has a definite approach to our life's work.

The Bible draws a parallel between "Bible study" and work.

With these two points in mind, let's look at the following scriptures:

Study to shew thyself approved unto God, a workman that needeth not to be ashamed, rightly dividing the word of truth.

2 Timothy 2:15 *KJV*

For the word of God is quick, and powerful, and sharper than any twoedged sword, piercing even to the dividing asunder of soul and spirit, and of the joints and marrow, and is a discerner [a critic] **of the thoughts and intents of the heart.**

Hebrews 4:12 *KJV*

All scripture is given by inspiration of God, and is profitable for doctrine, for reproof, for correction, for instruction in righteousness.

2 Timothy 3:16 *KJV*

For as he thinks in his heart, so is he....

Proverbs 23:7

First, let me stress this point: *What we believe about ourselves will determine the outcome of our lives.* That means we are personally responsible for our future.

There is nothing in your past that you can't overcome. There is no demonic attack so exclusively focused on you that you can't successfully resist it. There is no unbelief so strong that it can hold you back from fulfilling the dream God has given you.

You must understand that your past has been wiped out and that no demon spirit has any power in you or over you. Simply put, absolutely *nothing* can hold you back from being who God said you already are. Opportunity is knocking at your door like never before, and that opportunity extends to your workplace.

The key to unlocking those doors of opportunity is in James 1:22 (*KJV*): **"But be ye doers of the word, and not hearers only, deceiving your own selves."** You see, if you only hear the Word but never apply what you have heard to your life, you are living in a pipe dream. You'll only see good things happen in your life and at your job as you become *a doer of the Word*.

The Greatest Hindrance To Success: Fear

I've often been asked, "What is the primary thing that keeps most people from becoming successful in their job or career?" I think I've figured out part of the answer. The main thing that can prevent a person from bringing his career dreams to pass in his life is *fear*.

Luke 21:26 says, **"Men's hearts failing them from fear and the expectation of those things which are coming on the earth...."** Men's hearts fail them for fear of things that are coming upon the earth.

81

In Proverbs 29:25, it says, **"The fear of man brings a snare, but whoever trusts in the Lord shall be safe."** If you will put your trust in the Lord and refuse to fear, you will be kept safe in every area of life, including the workplace. As David wrote in Psalm 118:6: **"The Lord is on my side; I will not fear. What can man do to me?"**

Maybe you've heard someone speak these words over and over again: "The Lord is on my side; I will not fear. What can man do to me?" If so, you can know automatically that a strong attack is coming against a person who speaks that way. He is facing obstacles that could ultimately destroy him if he allowed them to.

If you are facing these types of obstacles, start saying what David said: *"The Lord is on my side; I refuse to fear!"*

- "I'm not going to fear anything my boss can do to me."

- "I'm not going to fear anything my coworker can do to me."

- "I'm not going to fear anything my customer or client can do to me."

- "I'm not going to fear what *any* person can do to me, for the Lord is on my side!"

How could David speak with such great confidence? How could he know for sure that God was going to take care of him? David discovered a place in God that most people never experience. It's a place where a believer in the Lord Jesus Christ can live, far above all the pulls, all the controls, and all the guilt trips of this life, continually shielded by God's grace.

In Psalm 91, which is actually one of the two psalms Moses wrote, verse 1 (*KJV*) says this: **"He that dwelleth**

in the secret place of the most High shall abide
under the shadow of the Almighty." Then notice
what verses 2 and 3 (*KJV*) say:

> I will say of the Lord, He is my refuge and my
> fortress: my God; in him will I trust.
> Surely he shall deliver thee from the snare of
> the fowler, and from the noisome pestilence.

God is going to deliver you from the noisome pesti-
lence. That isn't just talking about deliverance from
bugs; it's talking about deliverance from pesky situations and pesky people as well!

Verse 4 (*KJV*) goes on to say, **"He shall cover thee
with his feathers, and under his wings shalt thou
trust: his truth shall be thy shield and buckler."**
God's Word will protect you and keep you steady.

God is your refuge and your fortress. That's where
you can live continually — hidden in the refuge or the
fortress of the Most High. He will cover you with His
feathers, and under His wings will you trust. His truth
will be your shield and your buckler, giving you the
strength and support you need to refuse to be conformed
to this world.

Let's look at a few more verses from Psalm 91:

> A thousand shall fall at thy side, and ten
> thousand at thy right hand; but it shall not come
> nigh thee....
> There shall be no evil befall thee, neither shall
> any plague come nigh thy dwelling....
> With long life will I satisfy him, and shew him
> my salvation.

> **Psalm 91:7,10,16 *KJV***

Negative things sometimes happen in life that cause
us to become what God never wanted us to be. Sadly,
many of these things happen at our place of employment.

Too often situations happen in our interactions with other people at work in which we are tempted, cheated, lied to, or humiliated. But God has made provision for us to walk continually in His divine protection — and that protection extends into the workplace.

Steps to Fulfilling Your Dreams At the Workplace

So what can you do to be more productive and fulfilled on the job? The following are steps you can take to help you reach this goal.

Number one: Don't be caught up in the world's mindset. For instance, just because the boss cheats on his wife, that doesn't mean it's all right for you to do it too. Just because a coworker steals tools from his workplace, that doesn't make it right for you to steal as well. Just because a friend cheats on an expense report, that doesn't mean you can justify doing the same thing yourself.

If we aren't careful, we can be taken in by the world's mindset, attitudes, and prejudices. You see, people adopt certain mindsets, attitudes, and prejudices about everything in life. But we have been called by God to live *above* the mindset, the controls, and the prejudices of this world. We have been called to live a life of integrity.

Number two: Live a transparent life of integrity before God. Your employer may never see you take those office supplies, but God will. Your employer may never know that you're being critical behind his back, but God will.

You might ask, "What should I do when coworkers and supervisors turn against me?"

I like to do what Jesus did when everyone turned against Him. He kept His eyes on His goal; He kept His mouth shut; and He kept moving straight ahead. In fact, even at Jesus' lowest point, as He hung in agony on a brutal Cross, He forgave those who wronged Him. Never once did Jesus compromise His integrity or His relationship with the Father because of someone else's flesh.

So whenever you feel hatred and a desire for revenge building up within you, always remember that *you get rid of it by living above it.* You free yourself of negative feelings by showing the world that your position in the Lord Jesus Christ is greater than your position here on this earth. No matter what anyone says, thinks, or tries to do to you, he or she can do nothing to pull you out of your position in Christ.

Consider John the Baptist. Jesus called His cousin John *the greatest prophet who ever lived.* Yet John was not only ridiculed by the church leaders and political bosses of his time, but he was also forced to preach his message alone in the wilderness or the desert. Nevertheless, multitudes of people went out into that desert to hear him and receive the message God had called him to preach. Clothed in crude garments and a rough manner, John the Baptist would stand there and declare to all who would listen, *"Repent, for the Kingdom of Heaven is at hand!"*

Our position in life is not determined by anyone but God. So when people come against us on the job or anywhere else, we must live above all of that. We must deal scripturally with people who come against us, speaking to them graciously and with sensitivity but in bold, uncompromising faith. We must tell them of the freedom we have found in the Lord Jesus Christ. We must share with them that the position we have been given by God is better than any position life could ever give us.

Years ago in my own personal experience, life dealt me a death blow. Life said I wasn't going to make it. Life said I was doomed to fail. But *God* said that greater is He who is in me than he who is in the world (1 John 4:4). *God* said that because I am born of Him, I overcome the world, and this is the victory that overcomes the world — *my faith* (1 John 5:4).

God made you and me winners. In Galatians 3:26-28, the Bible tells us how:

> **For you are all sons of God through faith in Christ Jesus.**
> **For as many of you as were baptized into Christ have put on Christ.**
> **There is neither Jew nor Greek, there is neither slave nor free, there is neither male nor female; for you are all one in Christ Jesus.**

You see, through redemption it doesn't matter what you are or where you came from. *In Christ there is neither slave nor free, male nor female.* That means no one can lord it over you anymore. That also means you must free yourself from a victim's mentality so God can work in you and through you.

It doesn't matter if you're handicapped; it doesn't matter if you lack money or skills. No matter what your problem is, all you need to be is a child of God through faith in the Lord Jesus Christ. Then you are Christ's as well as Abraham's seed, and that makes you an heir according to the promise.

Don't let anyone in your life tell you that you were not made to win or that you are unworthy to win. *God has called you to win.* He has created you to be a God-bearer — a bearer of the One who created the universe with the words of His mouth. Therefore, it doesn't matter what anyone at the job says about you or thinks about you. It doesn't matter that others say you're at a disadvantage.

It doesn't matter what anyone else says or thinks. The only thing that matters is what God thinks — and He thinks you're a winner!

So maintain your position of integrity before God, no matter what anyone else says or does. Don't spend all your energy trying to defend yourself. Just trust in the Lord to move on your behalf, and you will come out the winner in every difficult situation you might encounter, both in the workplace and in every area of life.

Number three: Become detail-oriented. Be a person who pays close attention to detail at your place of employment. For example, when you walk down an aisle at work and see a piece of paper on the floor, pick it up off the floor yourself. Don't think, *I'm just going to leave that on the floor. After all, it's job security for the maintenance crew!*

You may think that something as small as picking up a piece of paper on the floor is insignificant, but this quality is actually very important to those in authority at the workplace. Employers look for employees who don't neglect the little details, such as being punctual. They know that a person who takes care of that one detail says a lot about his worth as an employee.

Number four, serve your employer with sincerity of heart. Of course you want to receive a promotion. Of course you want to make more money. But let me tell you something: Your employer doesn't have a problem with giving you more money. He has a problem if you think you are worth more money but have shown no proof of it in your performance on the job. *Job performance and attitude, not money, are the primary issues for most employers!*

You see, the first thing most people want to know these days when they are hired for a new job is "What is in it for me?"

- "How much will I get paid?

- "How much vacation do I get?"

- "How many sick days do I get?"

- "What holidays do I get off?"

- "How's the insurance package?"

But when you go to work as a Christian, you are primarily there to be a blessing.

When I worked at the largest and most successful parcel delivery company in the world, I loved my job. In my estimation, it was one of the greatest companies I could ever work for. I enjoyed every moment on that job.

One of the first things I did when I started working at this company was to go to my employer, my supervisors, and my managers and tell each of them, "I just want you to understand one thing, Sir. I'm here for the express purpose of getting you a promotion."

I hadn't been working at the time I applied for this job. I had no job, no money, no experience with that kind of work, *nothing*. But I went to this company anyway and filled out an application.

The application asked 150 questions on the back. The first question was "Have you ever been on drugs?"

I wrote down my honest but incriminating answer: *"Yes."*

"Have you ever had a bad back?"

"Yes."

"When was the last time your back hurt?"

"Today."

"Have you ever had mental problems?"

"Yes."

"Have you ever been institutionalized?"

"Yes."

Despite the fact that I had written down all the wrong answers, the interviewer looked at me and said, "Okay, you're hired. However," he added, "you'll have to shave your beard off."

When I heard that, I didn't complain or start a class-action suit. My only question to the man was "Do you have a razor?"

So I started the job and found out that I really enjoyed it. In fact, I loved it! I didn't love it because it was fun; I loved it because I was working unto God. Every time I went out delivering packages to the places they needed to go, I spent my time telling God, "I love You, Jesus! I'm here because I love You, and I know You love me!"

After the Christmas rush, the company laid me off. The boss told me, "Well, you know, maybe in February or March or April we'll call you back."

But I didn't wait for the company to call me. I called *them* — twice a week! I would tell the supervisor: "I just want to let you know one thing. I came here to work for your company because I'm good for you. I'm here to make you money. I can bring your company further along than it was before. I just want to let you know that you will never have one second of problem with me. I will be there to be part of your answer, not to be part of your problem."

You see, I didn't care if I got promoted. I wasn't working for my promotion. I wasn't trying to be good so I could get ahead. I was there to help my superiors receive a promotion. I was working for them because of my love for God.

In Ephesians 6:5, Paul says this:

> **Bondservants, be obedient to those who are your masters according to the flesh, with fear and trembling, in sincerity of heart, as to Christ.**

You are to serve your employer in sincerity of heart. However, that verse is referring to your sincere heart toward the Lord Jesus Christ, not toward your boss.

My sincerity wasn't toward my bosses when I worked at that delivery company; it was toward God. Otherwise, I couldn't have served them the way I did.

You see, when you become this kind of employee, your employer may not understand. He may even make fun of you. He may think, *Man, this guy is not real. No one is like this!* Then he may try to overwork you to see if he can break you or make you react negatively.

I recall one day when I had so much work, I was starting to get paranoid. That was one of those times my supervisor said, *"Thompson, I'm going to bury you with work."*

I replied, "Excuse me, Sir, but do you realize that you don't have enough work or enough trucks to bury me? Have a great day!"

Remember, there is a place of divine protection where you and I are to live continually. I'm talking about the secret place of the Most High, that dwelling place under the shadow of His wing. Despite opposition, I was supernaturally protected at my job, and so will you be protected at *your* workplace when you work as unto the Lord. God said so in His Word!

Number five: Pray for your supervisors. Spend an extra amount of time praying for your supervisors to get a promotion. If they are difficult to work for, allow God to promote them right out of your life! Ask God to bless them, and then stay available to minister to them at the workplace. Say from your heart, "I'm going to do my work as unto You, Father, and I know what that is going to do. It will ultimately bless my supervisor's socks off. In fact, it will bless him right out of here!"

Pray this from your heart: "Father, this man stands in the way of Your will. Save him or move him. But, please, Lord, move him up, not down." You see, bitterness moves a person down; blessing moves him up.

Ephesians 6:8 tells you what will happen in your life if you make a practice of blessing your employer:

...Whatever good anyone does, he will receive the same from the Lord, whether he is a slave or free.

In other words, as you make a practice of blessing your employer, you will be blessed as well!

So focus on fulfilling Colossians 3:17,23 at your job, and watch how God starts blessing you in return:

And whatever you do in word or deed, do all in the name of the Lord Jesus, giving thanks to God the Father through Him....
And whatever you do, do it heartily, as to the Lord and not to men.

Let me say a final word about blessings and prosperity in the workplace. *You should really stay away from seeking money.* If you seek money above seeking God's will for your life, it will destroy you. It will turn your focus the wrong way.

Have you found out God's will for your life? Is it God's will for your life to be paymaster in the Kingdom of God?

Is it God's will that you become a tremendous blessing as a businessperson and hire a number of people? If that is God's will for you, friend, you have to go in that direction.

But don't pursue that direction for the sake of money. Money will come. But your responsibility is to focus on being an answer to someone's problems, not just a courteous money-grabber.

Don't ever let anyone tell you that God isn't interested in your work or career. He *is* interested, and He wants you to experience the same kind of success and fulfillment on the job that you are destined to experience in every other area of your life.

Employers come and go, but God and His Word will never fail nor let you down. *So never let it be said that you didn't do your best on the job or that you didn't do your work as unto the Lord.* When you begin working from that perspective, the quality of your work and your attitude on the job will dramatically change for the better, and you will put yourself in position for your dreams of promotion to ultimately be fulfilled.

That's the goal of this book: To get you in position for the dreams God has placed in your heart to be restored and realized at last — even the ones that were shattered, crushed, or trampled on in the past. So take all these principles to heart that I've shared with you, and diligently apply every guideline to your life. And as you get in position for the success you've always longed for, always remember what it takes to overcome the "dream-destroyers":

Dream your dreams with integrity of heart.

Dream your dreams with faithfulness of mind.

Dream your dreams
through the skillfulness of your hands.

ACTION POINTS FOR REALIZING YOUR DREAM

- Realize that what you believe determines the outcome of your life.

- Don't be caught in the world's mindset!

- Live a transparent life of integrity before God.

- Become detailed-oriented at your job.

- Pray for your supervisors.

- Don't go after money. Instead, go after God's will through your relationship with Jesus Christ.

PRAYER OF SALVATION

Perhaps you have never been born again and there-fore haven't even begun to pursue the fulfillment of God-given dreams. If you have never received Jesus Christ as your personal Lord and Savior and would like to do that right now, just pray this simple prayer:

Dear Lord Jesus, I know that I am lost and need Your forgiveness. I believe that You died for me on the Cross and that God raised You from the dead. I now invite You to come into my heart to be my Lord and Savior. Forgive me of all sin in my life and make me who You want me to be. Amen.

If you prayed this prayer from your heart, congratu-lations! You have just changed your destiny and will spend eternity with God. Your sins were forgiven the moment you made Jesus the Lord of your life. Now God sees you as pure and holy, as if you had never sinned. You have been set free from the bondage of sin!

God didn't call you to live a life of mediocrity.
He didn't create you to be "just good enough."

These books will guide you down the road to excellence
so that you can experience the extraordinary
and bask in God's best.
Make the quality decision to pursue
His standard of excellence in every area of your life!

ROBB THOMPSON ROBB THOMPSON ROBB THOMPSON

$5 #4023/Soft Cover $10 #4026/Soft Cover $25 #4024/Hard Cover

Order Today!

Charge Orders, Call:	Europe Orders:	U.S. Orders:
United States	Winning in Life	Winning in Life
1-800-622-0017	Box 12	18500 92nd Avenue
Europe	266 Banbeury Rd	Tinley Park, IL 60477
(+44) 0-1865-553-920	Oxford OX27DL England	

OTHER BOOKS
BY ROBB THOMPSON

Victory Over Fear

The Winning Decision

You Are Healed

Marriage From God's Perspective

The Great Exchange:
Your Thoughts for God's Thoughts

Winning the Heart of God

Excellence in the Workplace

Excellence in Ministry

For a complete listing of additional products
by Robb Thompson, please call:

1-877-WIN-LIFE
(1-877-946-5433)

You can also visit us on the web at:
www.winninginlife.org

To contact Robb Thompson, please write:

Robb Thompson
P. O. Box 558009 Chicago, Illinois 60655

Please include your prayer requests
and comments when you write.